In the Night, Still Dark

by Richard Lewis
illustrated by Ed Young

Atheneum   1988   New York

This poem is an extensive abridgement of the first part of the Hawaiian creation chant called The Kumulipo. In its original version the chant was over two thousand lines long and was not only a record of the genealogies of the Kings, but also was chanted for the birth of each royal child in Hawaii. The Polynesians believed we are all a part of each living creature. The reason for chanting The Kumulipo after the birth of a child was to meld this bond of human life with the very first stirrings of life itself. On another level, this chant is a deeply insightful portrayal of an indigenous people's concept of evolution, and the eventual emergence of daylight.

Darkness of the sun, darkness of the night,
nothing but night.

In this the darkest night, in this the darkest sea,
After the coral was born, there came the mud-digging grub,
and its child, the earth worm.
There came the pointed star-fish, and the rock-grasping barnacle,
and its child, the oyster,
and its child, the mussel.

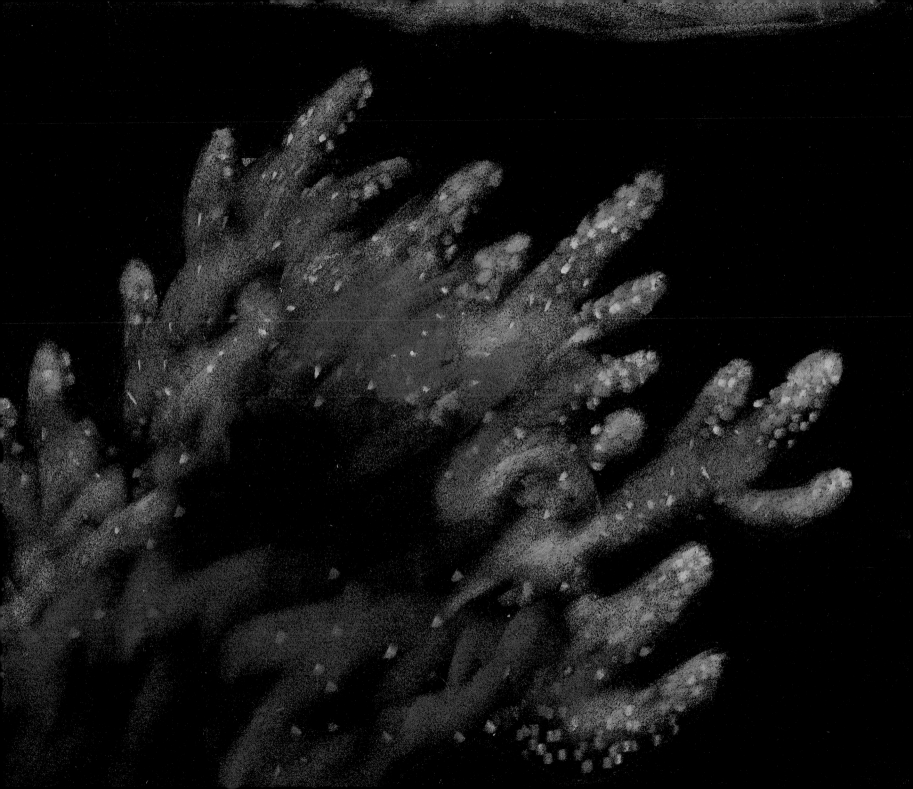

There came the moss which lives in the sea,
And the ferns which grow on the land,

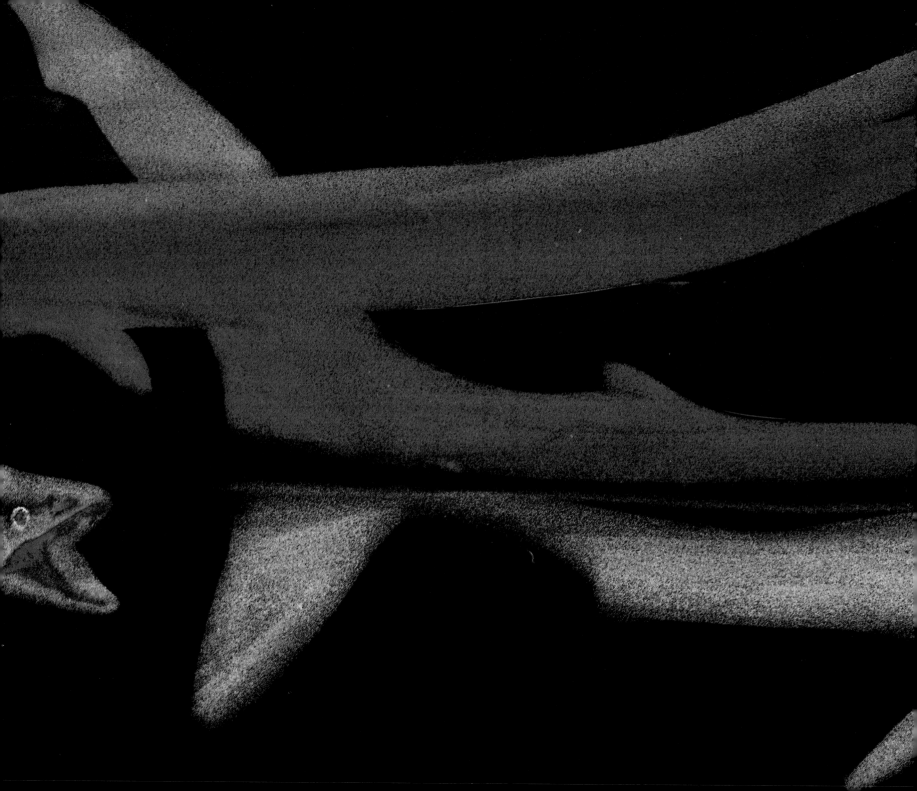

In this the darkest night
There came the fish, and all the creatures of the sea.
There came the lurking shark, and the darting eel,
　　　　moving quickly through the high weeds.

There came the stinging ray, and the hiding octopus,
waiting shyly in the deep waters.
There came all the creatures who swim, rise and dive,
swallowing, swallowing,
as they go.

In this the darkest night
The darkest night just breaking into dawn,
There came all the small, weak, and
                    flying things.
There came the furred caterpillar,
                    and its child, the moth.

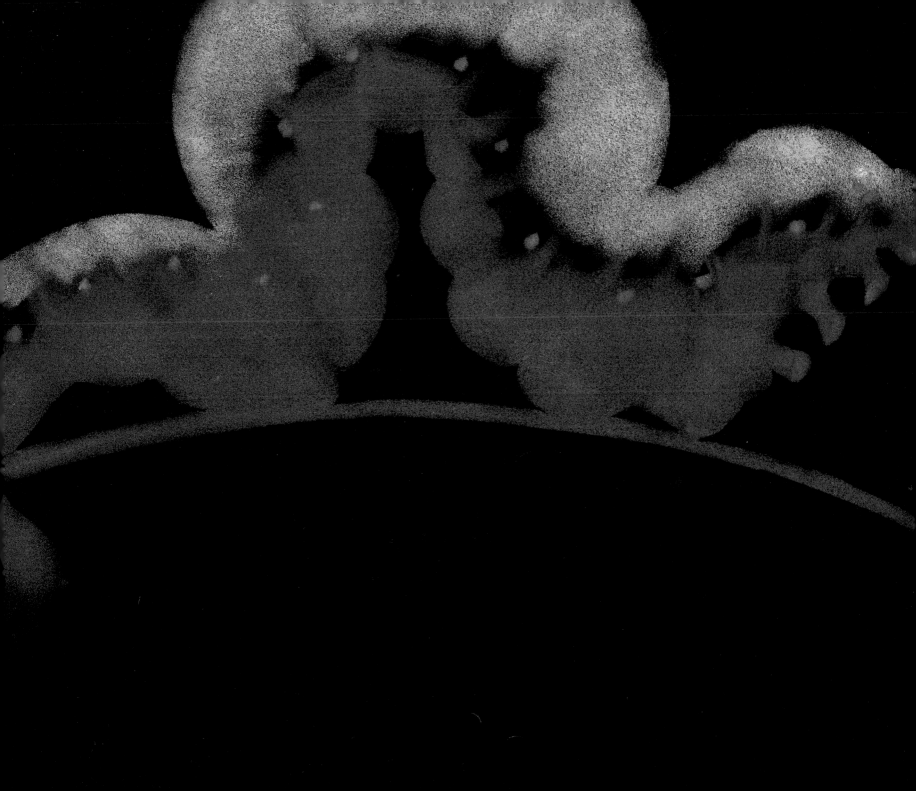

There came the scurrying ant,
and its child, the dragonfly.

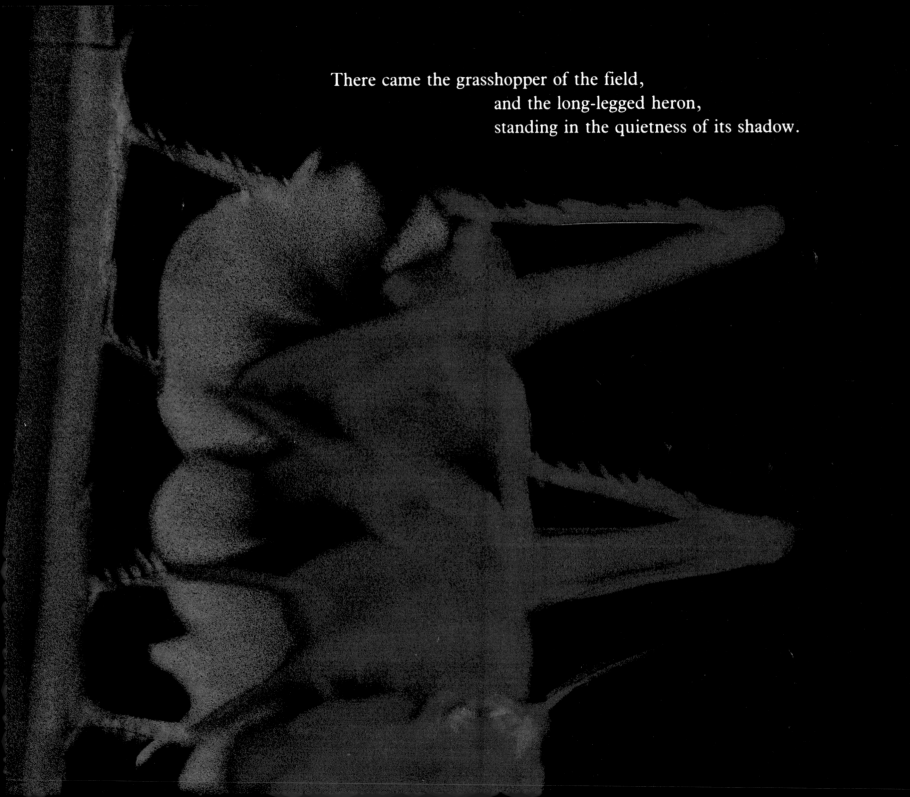

There came the grasshopper of the field,
and the long-legged heron,
standing in the quietness of its shadow.

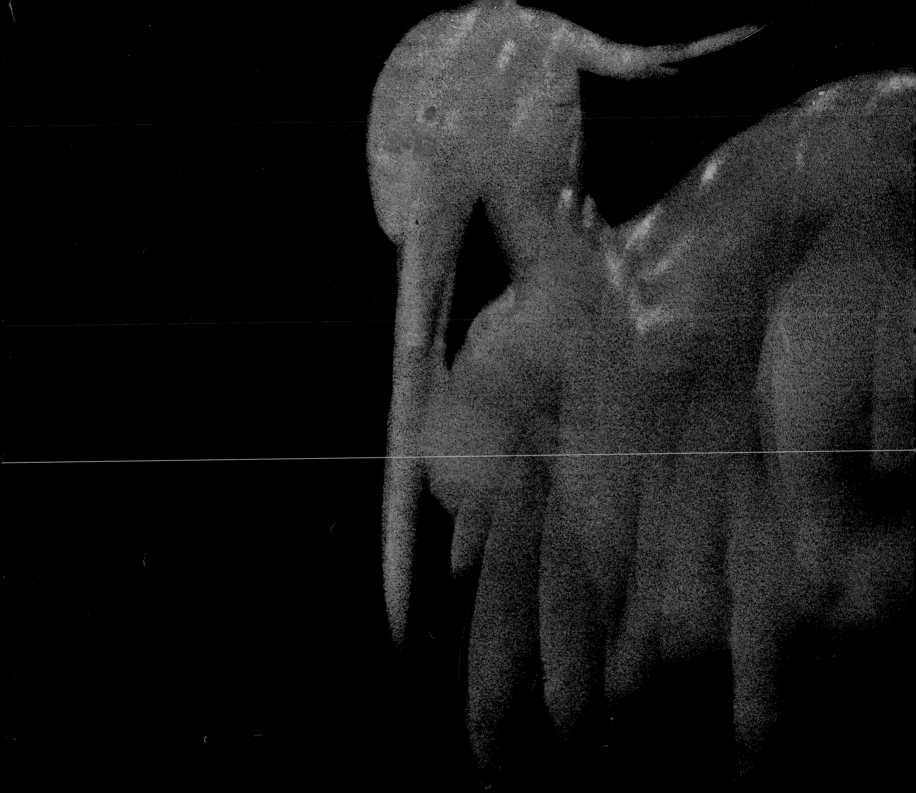

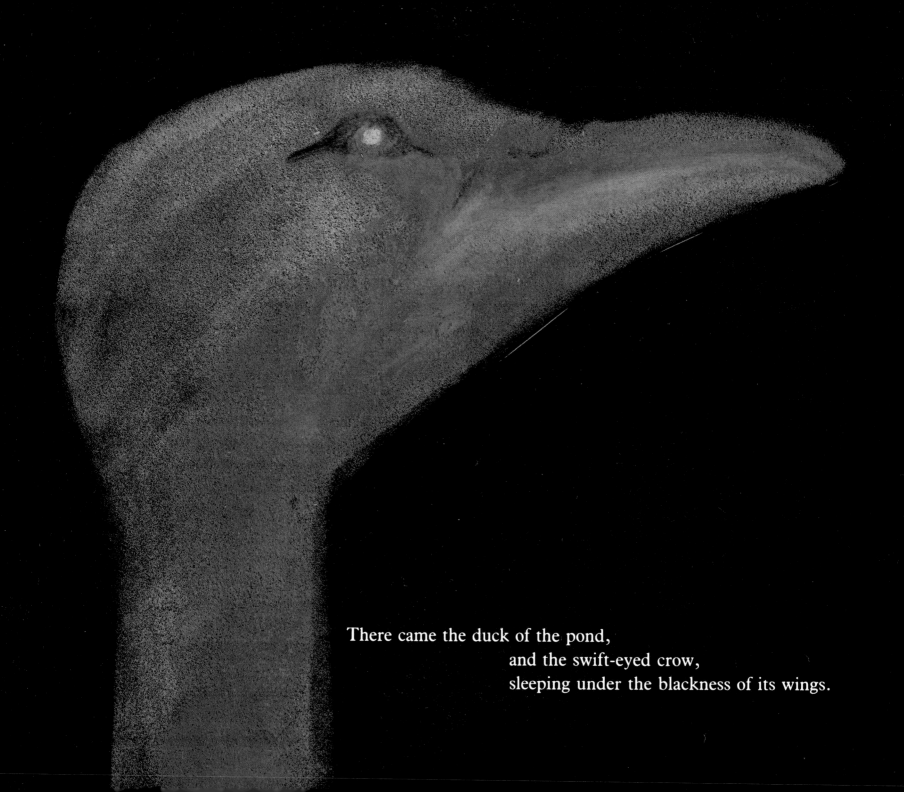

There came the duck of the pond,
and the swift-eyed crow,
sleeping under the blackness of its wings.

In this the darkest night,
The darkest night falling away,
The darkest night creeping away,
There came the rat who runs, here and there,
                    and with him the hairless red dog.

And out of the slime, roots began to grow.
Leaves began to branch.
And a great calmness,

And a great stillness
                came about.
And in this time men and women
                began to be born.

Here on the ocean's edge,
Here in the damp forest,
Here in the cold mountains,
People spread over the land.
People were here,
And so it was:

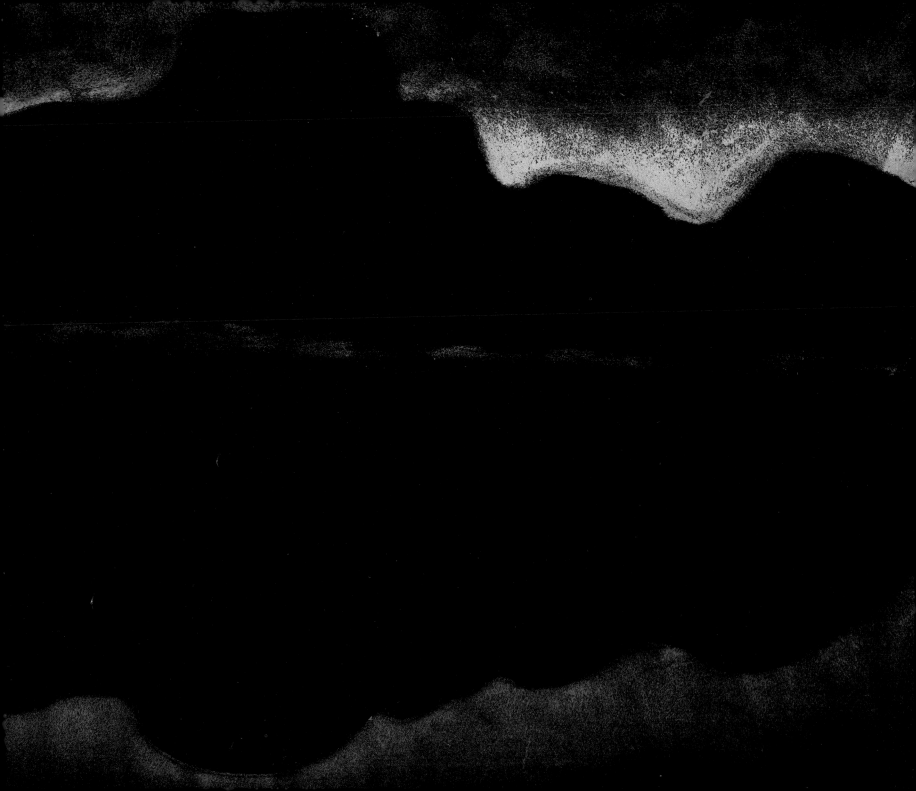

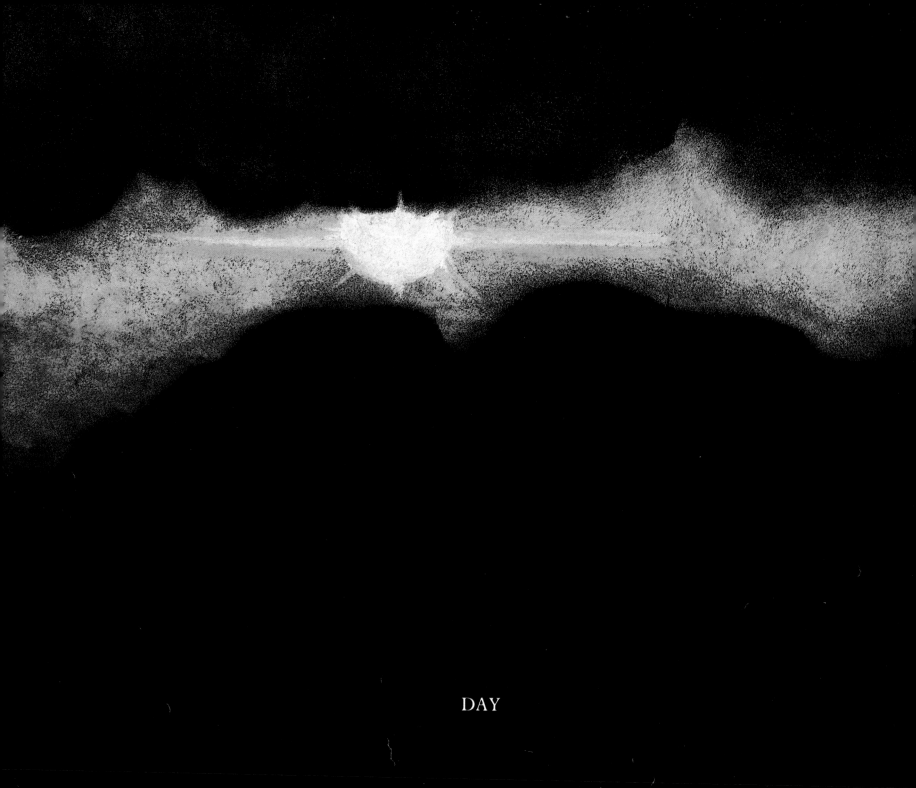

DAY

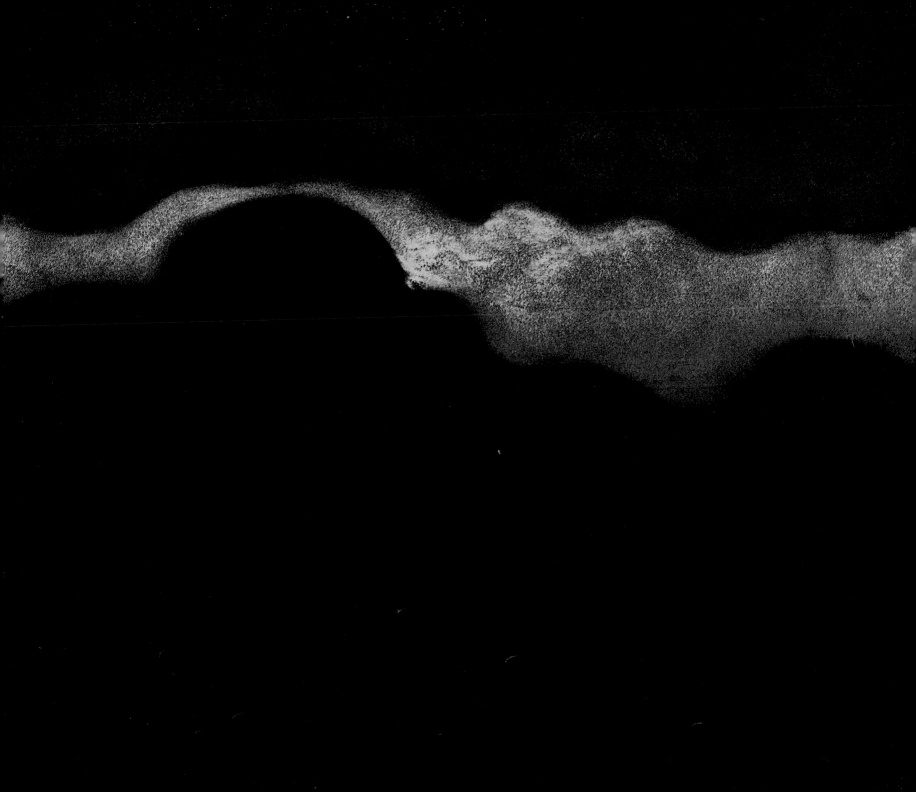

To those, who, listening
along the shores of their imagination, first
heard this poem of their beginnings.

(Richard Lewis)

To my mother, Tang Yün

(Ed Young)

The author would like to acknowledge that the text for *In the Night, Still Dark* was based on a shorter version of *The Kumulipo* that appeared in *In the Beginning: Creation Myths Around the World* by Maria Leach (Funk and Wagnalls Company, New York, 1956). Ms. Leach based her version on a translation of the original chant that appeared in *The Kumulipo: A Hawaiian Creation Chant* by Martha Beckwith (The University of Chicago Press, 1951).

Atheneum
Macmillan Publishing Company
866 Third Avenue, New York, NY 10022
Collier Macmillan Canada, Inc.

Type set by V & M Graphics, New York City
Printed and bound by the South China Printing Company, Hong Kong
First Edition
10 9 8 7 6 5 4 3 2 1

Library of Congress Cataloging-in-Publication Data

Lewis, Richard
  In the night, still dark.

  SUMMARY: A poetic description of how in the darkest night were born the simplest creatures, then with the breaking of dawn more complex ones, and finally people and day.
  1. Creation—Juvenile poetry. 2. Children's poetry, American. [1. Creation—Poetry]
I. Young, Ed, ill. II. Title.
PS3562.E972I5   1988   811'.54   87-11538
ISBN 0-689-31310-1